PARALLEL LIVES

FRED KOREMATSU

Born in 1919

JACKIE ROBINSON

Julie Knutson

CHERRY LAKE PRESS

Published in the United States of America by Cherry Lake Publishing
Ann Arbor, Michigan
www.cherrylakepublishing.com

Reading Adviser: Marla Conn, MS, Ed., Literacy specialist, Read-Ability, Inc.
Cover Designer: Felicia Macheske

Photo Credits: © Shirley Nakao/Courtesy of the Fred T. Korematsu Institute, cover, 1 [left]; © National Archives/U.S. Information Agency/Identifier 6802718, cover, 2 [right]; © Everett Historical/Shutterstock.com, 5, 8, 11, 21; © Library of Congress, LC-USF33-012696-M2, 6; © Library of Congress, LC-DIG-stereo-1s10222, 7; © Courtesy of the Fred T. Korematsu Institute, 12; © Library of Congress, LC-USZ62-133633, 14; © Shirley Nakao/Courtesy of the Fred T. Korematsu Institute, 16; © Hulton Archive/Getty Images, 19; © Library of Congress, LC-USW33-038539-ZC, 22; © Ray Howard/Associated Press, 24; © Bettmann/Getty Images, 25; © Jerry Coli/Dreamstime.com, 26

Library of Congress Cataloging-in-Publication Data

Names: Knutson, Julie, author.
Title: Born in 1919 : Fred Korematsu and Jackie Robinson / by Julie Knutson.
Description: Ann Arbor : Cherry Lake Publishing, [2020] | Series: Parallel lives | Includes index. | Audience: Grades 4-6
Identifiers: LCCN 2019033449 | ISBN 9781534159198 (hardcover) | ISBN 9781534161498 (paperback) | ISBN 9781534160347 (pdf) | ISBN 9781534162648 (ebook)
Subjects: LCSH: United States—Social conditions—20th century—Juvenile literature. | United States—Race relations—20th century—Juvenile literature. | Korematsu, Fred, 1919-2005—Juvenile literature. | Japanese Americans—Evacuation and relocation, 1942-1945—Juvenile literature. | Japanese Americans—Civil rights—History—20th century—Juvenile literature. | Civil rights workers—United States—Biography—Juvenile literature. | Japanese Americans—Biography—Juvenile literature. | Robinson, Jackie, 1919-1972—Juvenile literature. | Baseball players—United States—Biography—Juvenile literature. | African American baseball players—United States—Biography—Juvenile literature.
Classification: LCC HN57 .K58 2020 | DDC 306.0973—dc23
LC record available at https://lccn.loc.gov/2019033449

Cherry Lake Publishing would like to acknowledge the work of the Partnership for 21st Century Learning, a Network of Battelle for Kids. Please visit www.battelleforkids.org/networks/p21 for more information.

Printed in the United States of America
Corporate Graphics

ABOUT THE AUTHOR

Julie Knutson shares a birth year with Venus Williams, Chelsea Clinton, and Lin-Manuel Miranda. An avid student of history and former teacher, she lives in northern Illinois with her husband and son.

TABLE OF CONTENTS

CHAPTER 1

Welcome to 1919

1919. American civil rights activist Fred Korematsu and American professional baseball player Jackie Robinson are born into a world recovering from the destruction of World War I (1914–1918). But that doesn't mean times were peaceful, especially in the United States. Workers across the country were on **strike** for higher wages and better working conditions. Fears about **terrorism** and disloyalty to America skyrocketed. In the years before and after 1919, many Americans faced very real threats to their safety because of their race or **ethnicity**.

Anti-Immigrant Policies: **Immigrants** and their children encountered **discrimination** in all aspects of their lives. The United States banned Chinese immigration in 1882 with the

World War I was called "the war to end all wars."

Many Chinese immigrants arrived in the United States for the gold rush that was taking place in California during the 1800s.

Chinese Exclusion Act. This law remained in effect until 1943. Asian immigrants from China, Japan, and Korea couldn't become **naturalized** citizens and were not welcomed into many communities. In states like California, **segregation** was widespread. Barbershops and restaurants regularly refused service to Asian American customers.

Angel Island Immigration Station is located in San Francisco, California. It operated from 1910 to 1940. It held and interrogated Asian immigrants.

Ku Klux Klan activity spiked in the early 1900s and continued throughout the civil rights movement.

Segregation and Jim Crow: In 1919, 83 African Americans were **lynched**. Many victims were soldiers who had recently returned from World War I. The Ku Klux Klan, which was active in 27 states, claimed responsibility for many of these murders. The National Association for the Advancement of Colored People (NAACP), an organization that promotes justice and civil rights for African Americans, urged lawmakers to put an end to lynching. Widespread race riots, sparked by white fears that black Americans would take their jobs, erupted in the late spring.

"Jim Crow" Laws

Jim Crow laws legalized segregation from the late 1800s to mid-1900s. They set different rules for black and white Americans. These laws were a reaction to freedoms given to African Americans during the period immediately after the Civil War.

CHAPTER 2

Fred Korematsu (b. January 30, 1919)

On December 7, 1941, Japanese planes attacked the U.S. military base at Pearl Harbor in Honolulu, Hawaii. More than 2,400 people were killed. Another 1,000 were wounded. The next day, the United States declared war on Japan and entered World War II. During the war, many white Americans grew suspicious of their Japanese neighbors, fearing they were spies who threatened national security. In response, President Franklin D. Roosevelt issued Executive Order 9066. It authorized the forced evacuation of Japanese Americans from California, Oregon, and Washington State to inland locations. Most went along with the order to show loyalty to the government, leaving behind homes, loved ones, and

Over 100,000 Japanese Americans were sent to live in internment camps across the western United States.

Fred and his family stand in their flower nursery in 1939.

businesses. But a few people stood up and challenged the idea that they weren't "American" because they were of Japanese descent.

Fred Korematsu was one of them.

Early Years: Finding a Voice

Fred was born on January 30, 1919, in Oakland, California. His birth name was Toyosaburo, but his first-grade teacher struggled to pronounce it. Instead, she called him Fred. Fred's parents were first-generation Japanese American immigrants, or *Issei*. They owned a flower nursery and were proud of their **heritage**. They celebrated traditional holidays and hired Japanese language tutors for their four sons. But Fred, who was ***Nisei***, considered himself more American than Japanese. He preferred speaking English. He participated in Scouts, ran track-and-field, and played tennis.

At school, Fred felt accepted. But outside of its walls, he endured discrimination and stares. This negative attention grew stronger in 1941, as America grew closer to entering the war. At the time, Fred was 22 years old, in love, and working full-time. He tried to enlist in the military but was denied.

Then came the attack on Pearl Harbor. Fear and hatred were growing—and the *Issei* and *Nisei* were targets.

Internment Camps

Over 100,000 Japanese Americans were forcibly relocated to remote ***internment*** *camps during World War II. After receiving government orders to move, families had to quickly determine what to do with their homes and businesses. They were allowed two suitcases per person. At first, they were housed at former racetracks and fairgrounds, often sleeping in horse stalls. They were later moved to guarded camps throughout the United States.*

The internment camps were overcrowded and most facilities lacked proper plumbing.

Middle Years: Expressing a Voice

When Executive Order 9066 went into effect, it required Japanese Americans to leave their homes and report to "assembly centers." Fred knew this wasn't fair and refused to obey the order. Instead, he rented a room and changed his name to disguise his ancestry.

Fred avoided capture for several weeks. But on May 30, 1942, he was arrested and jailed. Reports of his arrest appeared in newspapers nationwide. A lawyer named Ernest Besig, from the American Civil Liberties Union, read one of the reports. He wanted to take on Fred's case as a test to see if he could fight the imprisonment of all Japanese Americans. Fred agreed. Ernest paid his **bail**, and Fred was released.

Unfortunately, release from jail didn't spell freedom for Fred. He was forced to report to the temporary prison camp where his family and thousands of other Japanese Americans were held. In September 1942, Fred and his family were moved to a more "permanent" camp in Utah. Many residents didn't welcome Fred. They thought that by fighting the government's orders, he made himself and all Japanese Americans seem disloyal. He wasn't thanked for his actions or labeled a hero. He was rejected.

Fred left the camp in December 1942 on a work permit. He moved first to Salt Lake City, Utah, and later to Detroit, Michigan. All the while, his legal case made its way through the court system. He followed its developments through letters from Ernest. In March 1944, the Supreme Court announced that it would hear Fred's case—*Korematsu v. United States*—in October.

In December 1944, while Fred's case was still before the Supreme Court, President Roosevelt canceled Executive Order 9066. After hearing the president's decision, the court reached their own. Six of the nine judges ruled in the government's favor, stating that the removal of Japanese Americans from their homes was legal. This meant that despite Japanese Americans being able to leave the camps, the fight wasn't over.

In 1998, Fred was awarded the Presidential Medal of Freedom.

Later Years: Leaving a Legacy

For the next 30-plus years, Fred lived a quiet life in Oakland, California, with his wife, Kathryn, and their children, Karen and Ken. Still, Fred's act of resistance impacted the rest of his life. Many jobs were closed to him because he'd been found guilty of committing a crime.

Meanwhile, law students continued to study *Korematsu v. United States* as a failure of **civil liberties**. In 1982, a researcher named Peter Irons reached out to Fred with new information. Peter uncovered evidence that officials had lied about the risk that Japanese Americans posed to national security. Peter proposed they reopen the case. Fred agreed to take on the government yet again. In 1983, a federal judge ruled in their favor, and Fred was cleared of all charges.

Fred Korematsu never stopped fighting for justice. Following the September 11, 2001, attacks, he repeated the message he'd stated for more than 55 years: "No one should ever be locked away simply because they share the same race, ethnicity, or religion as a spy or terrorist."

Reparations

In 1988, the U.S. government passed the Civil Liberties Act. It promised $20,000 in **reparations** *to each Japanese American survivor of internment. Survivors received the payment in October 1990.*

CHAPTER 3

Jackie Robinson (b. January 31, 1919)

Jackie Robinson didn't just change baseball—he changed American culture. In 1947, Robinson became the first African American player in Major League Baseball (MLB) in the modern era. Before then, the sport was segregated into the all-black Negro League and the all-white Major Leagues. At his first Major League game, Jackie faced taunts, threats, and jeers from white fans and other players. How did he find the courage to keep playing? He drew on years of fighting segregation in every part of his life to prove that all Americans deserved to work and play on the same field.

Jackie Robinson's full name is Jack Roosevelt Robinson. He was named after U.S. President Theodore Roosevelt.

Early Years: Finding a Voice

Jackie Robinson found his voice early in life. As a black child in a white, working-class neighborhood in Pasadena, California, he experienced racial discrimination firsthand. A cross was burned on the family's lawn. Neighbors tried to buy his mother's house to get the family to leave. Others called the police to complain about the noise that Jackie's brother made while roller-skating. But the family stayed, and Jackie spoke out against racism at every opportunity.

Like Fred, Jackie lived in a segregated, Jim Crow-era California. Black, Asian, and Latino kids could only swim in the community pool during a 3-hour window on Wednesdays. Then, the pool was drained, cleaned, and refilled for white swimmers. Movie theaters and restaurants were segregated. As a teen, Jackie found ways to challenge segregation. He snuck into the white section of the theater after the lights dimmed. He once sat at a lunch counter until he and his friends were served. He never passively accepted segregation.

African Americans in World War II

World War II put human rights issues in the United States and abroad in the spotlight. Black soldiers defended freedom and democracy in Europe, only to return home and be treated unfairly. During the war, African Americans at home contributed to all aspects of the cause, from growing **victory gardens** *to working in the defense industry. Civil rights activists pointed out this* **contradiction***. While African Americans fulfilled their citizenship duties with honor, they still didn't enjoy full equality. This sparked the movement to eliminate segregation in all aspects of American life.*

Over 2.5 million African Americans signed up to fight in World War II. The U.S. military remained segregated throughout the war.

The attack on Pearl Harbor is often referred to as "a date which will live in infamy." The phrase is from a speech by President Franklin D. Roosevelt.

Jackie was an outstanding athlete and played four sports while at the University of California, Los Angeles (UCLA). He was 1 of only 50 black students on a campus of 9,600. While his athletic abilities drew cheering crowds, unspoken rules on campus said that he couldn't attend parties. Written rules said that he couldn't even live near campus, as the neighborhoods surrounding it were white-only.

Jackie left UCLA 3 months before graduating. The United States was still in the Great Depression, and Jackie landed a job as a construction worker at Pearl Harbor in Hawaii. He worked at Pearl Harbor until December 5, 1941, 2 days before it was bombed. Jackie was drafted into the U.S. Army on March 23, 1942.

Middle Years: Expressing a Voice

Jack reported for duty. He did very well in training and was eager to advance. But discrimination kept him from being accepted to the base's Officer Candidate School (OCS). With the help of friends, he fought back and was admitted to OCS. Throughout his time in the military, he battled segregation. When he refused to move to the back of a military bus, he was **court-martialed**. He didn't back down and spoke his truth at the trial. He was **acquitted**.

Jackie went to six World Series with the Dodgers.

After he was released from the military, Jackie joined the Negro American League, a professional baseball league for African Americans. While he was playing shortstop for the Kansas City Monarchs, other Americans were working to desegregate baseball. Sportswriters, politicians, and labor organizers pushed to see change. They needed someone strong to be the first to **integrate** the sport.

Jackie joined the Brooklyn Dodgers in 1945. The team's owner, Branch Rickey, warned Jackie that the path wouldn't be easy. Jackie would have to live with physical and verbal abuse. He needed to stay calm, avoid conflict, and not fight back on the field. For a

Jackie Robinson was elected into the National Baseball Hall of Fame in 1962.

Jackie Robinson's jersey number, 42, is retired in honor of his memory.

person who had spoken against discrimination his entire life, this would be a challenge. But Jackie accepted. He played one season in the minor leagues for the Montreal Royals. He played his first Major League game on April 15, 1947.

Jackie wasn't warmly received by all of his teammates. Other Dodgers started a **petition** to keep him off the field. The Philadelphia Phillies and Saint Louis Cardinals threatened to strike if Jackie played. He endured hate on and off the field. But he persisted. He was a top base stealer and home run hitter in his first season, leading the Dodgers to the World Series. By the end of 1947, polls showed that he was one of the most respected men in America.

Later Years: Leaving a Legacy

Jackie's career with the Dodgers lasted 10 years. In that decade, baseball continued to desegregate. Through the actions of courageous people, the sport—and the broader world—was beginning to change.

After he left baseball, Jackie used his voice to advocate for equal rights within and beyond the black community. He worked to create financial opportunities for African Americans by co-founding the Freedom National Bank in New York. He pushed for school integration alongside Dr. Martin Luther King Jr. Whether in baseball, business, or education, Jackie fought to erase color lines and build a world with full equality for all people.

Jackie Robinson Day

Every April 15, Major League Baseball observes Jackie Robinson Day. On this day, everyone on the field—players, coaches, managers, and umpires—wear the number 42 to honor Jackie's memory.

1919

January 30, 1919
Fred Korematsu is born in California.

January 31, 1919
Jackie Robinson is born in Georgia.

1939

1939
Jackie transfers from Pasadena City College to UCLA on an athletic scholarship.

1940

December 7, 1941
Japan bombs the American military base at Pearl Harbor.

February 19, 1942
President Roosevelt signs Executive Order 9066.

March 1942
Jackie is drafted into the U.S. Army.

May 30, 1942
Fred is arrested in Oakland, California, for violating Executive Order 9066.

December 1944
The Supreme Court rules against Fred in *Korematsu v. United States*.

December 1944
President Roosevelt cancels Executive Order 9066. Japanese Americans start to be released.

1945
Jackie joins the Kansas City Monarchs in the Negro Leagues.

March 1946
The last Japanese internment camp is closed.

April 15, 1947
Jackie is MLB's first African American player in the modern era.

1949
Jackie is named MLB's Most Valuable Player.

1957
Jackie retires from baseball.

1962
Jackie is inducted into Baseball's Hall of Fame.

1965
Jackie co-founds the Freedom National Bank.

1972
Jackie dies at his home in Connecticut.

1983
A federal judge overrules Fred's conviction.

October 1990
Japanese American survivors of internment camps receive monetary reparations from the U.S. government.

1998
Bill Clinton bestows the Presidential Medal of Freedom on Fred.

2005
Fred dies at his home in California.

1957 1960 1972 1983 1990 2005

Research and Act

Many people still face prejudice today. Activists continue in the tradition of Fred Korematsu and Jackie Robinson to disrupt discrimination and promote justice.

Research

People of all ages work together to break down barriers based on race, ethnicity, gender, and religion in their communities. In 2001, Teaching Tolerance launched a campaign called the Mix It Up at Lunch Day to do just this in school settings.

Visit the official Mix It Up website at https://www.tolerance.org/mix-it-up and think about the following: Why was Mix It Up started? Who benefits from this program? Where and when does it happen? How does it build more tolerant schools?

Act

Talk to teachers and administrators in your school about Mix It Up. Work with peers to petition for a Mix It Up at Lunch Day at your school. And don't wait until the "official" day to make a difference! You can "mix it up" at any point in the year by sitting with someone new in the cafeteria.

Further Reading

Atkins, Laura. *Fred Korematsu Speaks Up.* Berkeley, CA: Heyday, 2017.

Kenney, Karen Latchana. *Korematsu v. the United States: World War II Japanese-American Internment Camps.* Minneapolis, MN: ABDO, 2013.

Rappaport, Doreen. *42 Is Not Just a Number: The Odyssey of Jackie Robinson, American Hero.* Somerville, MA: Candlewick Press, 2017.

Williams, Heather. *Jackie Robinson.* Ann Arbor, MI: Cherry Lake Publishing, 2019.

GLOSSARY

acquitted (uh-KWIT-id) cleared of wrongdoing or a criminal charge

bail (BAYL) money paid to a court for the release of someone accused of a crime, with the promise that the person will show up for their trial

civil liberties (SIV-uhl LIB-ur-teez) freedom from government interference based on opinions rather than reason

contradiction (kahn-truh-DIK-shuhn) actions or conditions that are opposed to each other

court-martialed (KORT MAHR-shuld) given a military trial

discrimination (dis-krim-ih-NAY-shuhn) unfair behavior to others based on differences in race or gender

ethnicity (eth-NIH-sih-tee) a group that shares the same national or cultural traditions

heritage (HER-ih-tij) traditions and beliefs that people consider an important part of their history

immigrants (IM-ih-gruhnts) people who move from one country to another and settle there

integrate (IN-tuh-grate) to include people of all races

internment (in-TURN-muhnt) prison that holds people for political or military reasons

lynched (LINCHD) killed by a mob without having had a legal trial

naturalized (NACH-ur-uh-lized) process for a foreign-born person to gain citizenship

Nisei (nee-SAY) second-generation Japanese American

petition (puh-TISH-uhn) a letter signed by many people telling those in power how they feel about a certain situation

reparations (rep-uh-RAY-shuhnz) payments for a past wrong

segregation (seg-rih-GAY-shuhn) the practice of keeping people or groups (such as racial or ethnic) apart

strike (STRIKE) a situation in which workers stop or refuse to work

terrorism (TER-uh-riz-uhm) the use of violence and threats in order to frighten people and obtain power

victory gardens (VIK-tor-ee GAHR-duhnz) gardens planted during wartime to increase food production

INDEX